Deborah and Jael

Warrior Women

by

Gwen R. Shaw

Engeltal Press
P.O. Box 447
Jasper, ARK 72641-0447
U.S.A.
www.engeltalpress.com

Cover illustration by Carolyn H. Wright

ISBN 0-9740588-9-0

Printed in the United States of America

DEBORAH, A WOMAN OF POWER, AUTHORITY AND HONOUR

Her name was Deborah. It means "bee." She was a woman of great courage and wisdom; and she had faith to do the impossible, and inspire others to do likewise. We do not know how old she was. But, whether she was young or old, we know that she gave honour to her people in a time when they had none. She inspired men, who were in the depths of despair, to have hope and rise again to greatness of courage and bravery, and to deliver themselves from the bondage and tyranny of one of history's most powerful and cruel tyrants that has ever ruled over an occupied nation. She saved Israel through the gift of prophecy.

Her life gave such honour to her name that for over three thousand years both Jewish and Christian mothers have named their daughters in her honour. Deborah will live forever in the annals of history, not only as one of Israel's greatest women, but as one of the greatest women of all time and all nations. For women everywhere she has become an eternal role model and reminder of what God can accomplish through one of us. Just to hear her name lifts our spirits and inspires us to pride and confidence, faith and courage not to give up, but to believe that God can use a woman to change the destiny of a nation.

This book is dedicated to Deborah, the Fourth Judge of Israel, and the only woman judge. She called herself *"a mother in Israel."*

GOD'S ORIGINAL PLAN WAS THAT ISRAEL SHOULD BE RULED BY JUDGES

In Deuteronomy 16:18-22, the Lord had given instruction through His servant Moses that when they settled in the land they were to have judges to keep order and peace among the people: "*Judges and officers shalt thou make thee in all thy gates, which the LORD thy God giveth thee, throughout thy tribes: and they shall judge the people with just judgment.*"

He told them that they were to be honest, and not change, nor turn away from laws of righteousness nor accept bribery; *"Thou shalt not wrest judgment; thou shalt not respect persons, neither take a gift: for a gift doth blind the eyes of the wise, and pervert the words of the righteous."*

He told the people that they must live righteous lives; *"That which is altogether just shalt thou follow, that thou mayest live, and inherit the land which the LORD thy God giveth thee."*

And finally He warned them against setting up a place they could turn into a center for idolatry; *"Thou shalt not plant thee a grove of any trees near unto the altar of the LORD thy God, which thou shalt make thee. Neither shalt thou set thee up any image; which the LORD thy God hateth."*

The judges had great responsibility to keep the people at peace with each other and faithful in their worship of God.

THE LAND OF MILK AND HONEY

There is a great mystery about Deborah. As I said, her name means a "bee." A bee is one of God's most precious gifts to man; it not only has the power to sting and make brave men run for their lives, it also has the ability to make honey. The humblest bee can participate in that great achievement. Honey delights the taste, and gives strength and health to the body. Dr. Thomas L. Constable, in his *Notes on Judges 2003 Edition*, states "Her name means 'Bee' and she did what most marks a bee. She stung the enemy, and she brought sweet refreshment to her people." There are times when the only way that you can deliver your people is by "stinging" the enemy! You can't be nice to everybody. In this marvellous story of the deliverance of Israel out of bondage it took two "gutsy" and cunning women to do what the men in their day were powerless to do. Fear had paralyzed the men of Israel, for they regarded their enemy, the Canaanites and their King Jabin, the king of the city of Hazor in Galilee and his powerful, cunning commander, Sisera, as impossible to defeat.

The Land of Promise was a land of *"milk and honey."* The Lord, Himself, called it that (Exodus 3:8,17; 13:5; 33:3; Leviticus 20:24); and this is repeated in Numbers and Deuteronomy many times. The Lord found a woman whom He could use to restore the sweetness and the strength of the Land.

The other woman whom God used was Jael. They tell us that her name means "wild goat." It was from goats that Israel got most of her milk in Bible times. Jael had her supply of milk, and she gave it to the powerful Commander of King Jabin's army, Sisera, to drink, thereby causing him to fall into a deep sleep, from which he never awoke. But we will read her story later in this book. So it is that God used two women to restore the milk and the honey to Israel—the Land of Milk and Honey!

WHAT MADE DEBORAH GREAT?

The King James Version of the story states, *"And Deborah, a prophetess, the wife of Lapidoth, she judged Israel at that time"* (Judges 4:4).

According to the King James Version we get the impression that Deborah was a married woman, and that her husband's name was Lapidoth. But I want to draw your attention to the fact that the Hebrew word for "wife," which is used here is *"ishshah"* (802 in Strong's Concordance), can also be interpreted, "woman" and "female." It is the same word used in Genesis 2:22-23, *"And the rib, which the LORD God had taken from man, made he a woman (ishshah), and brought her unto the man. And Adam said, This is now bone of my bones, and flesh of my flesh: she shall be called Woman (ishshah), because she was taken out of Man*" (iysh).

The word "Lapidoth" (3940) in Hebrew is interpreted "to shine, lamp, flame, burning lamp, lightning, torch."

Therefore, this verse could also be interpreted, "And Deborah, a prophetess, **a woman of light**, judged Israel at that time" instead of, "*And Deborah, a prophetess, **the wife of Lapidoth**, she judged Israel at that time.*"

Matthew Henry's Commentary on the subject says the terminology, "'*the wife of Lapidoth'* is not commonly found in connection with a man. Some make this the name of a place: she was *a woman of Lapidoth.* Others take it as meaning, Lapidoth signifies *'lamps.'* Some Bible scholars say she had employed herself in making wicks for the lamps of the tabernacle; and having stooped to that mean office for God, she was afterwards thus preferred. Or she was a woman of *illuminations,* or of *splendours*, one extraordinarily known and wise, and so came to be very eminent and illustrious." Henry goes on to say that she was intimately acquainted with God, she was a prophetess, and one that instructed others in divine knowledge by the inspiration of the Spirit of God, and had gifts of wisdom, to which she attained not in an ordinary way; she *heard the words of God,* and probably *saw the visions of the Almighty*. She was totally devoted to Israel. After Jehovah, Israel was her first love."

That Deborah was a "woman of light" we can have no doubt. She was a daughter of Israel, a woman of great righteousness and excellence, who received her illumination and wisdom from the One Who is THE LIGHT OF THE WORLD. That was the same LIGHT that shone in the dwellings of the Israelites back in Egypt when darkness was over all the land, and the same Light gave revelation to Israel when they were in the wilderness.

God grant that we women, who say we are followers of the One True God, also become Women of Light in a day when there is so much darkness on every side, and mankind gropes in darkness to find the way. Jesus said *"Ye are the light of the world"* (Matthew 5:14).

In Isaiah 60: 1-3 we read the encouraging prophetic word for our time, *"Arise, shine; for thy light is come, and the glory of the LORD is risen upon thee. For, behold, the darkness shall cover the earth, and gross darkness the people: but the LORD shall arise upon thee, and his glory shall be seen upon thee. And the Gentiles shall come to thy light, and kings to the brightness of thy rising."*

It is in times of calamity that God raises up His great champions of faith, like Joseph, Moses, Gideon, Sampson, Deborah, Esther, the Blessed Virgin Mary, Joan of Arc, Winston Churchill, and many others. Will some of you who are reading this book be the Lord's champion for your generation? If you are, it will cost you everything!

Although it is believed by some students of ancient history that Deborah was a woman of wealth, I do not believe she was. She appeared to possess no special privileges, but sat out in the open air under a palm tree, and the people came to her from all over the land to tell her about their troubles and to ask for counsel. She never charged for her counsel, though it occupied much of her time. She it was who judged the people and settled disputes among them. She was the "Solomon" of her day. People respected and honoured her. Her wisdom was not of this world. Her ear was tuned to the High Council of Heaven, and it was from thence that her wisdom came, providing wisdom and guidance for the present, and the future.

There are many things that can make a woman great. One of them is the times in which she is born. Let us look into Deborah's era.

WHAT HAD CAUSED ISRAEL TO LOSE HER GREATNESS?

Deborah lived at a time when the older generation, the pioneers and "Lions of faith" had all died out. They had been the ones who had seen the mighty works of God, and still remembered the miracles of their deliverance from Egypt, their struggle in the howling Wilderness for forty long years, their victorious crossing of both the Red Sea, and later the Jordan River, into The Promised Land, and most of all, the time when God Almighty, Himself, had come down from Heaven upon the great Mountain in the Desert and visited them. They would never forget the sound of His thunder, the roaring of the Heavens, the shaking of the mountain, and the fire of His Presence. They had looked down at the desert sands under their feet, and knew that they were standing on Holy Ground, and their surrounding world was the Temple of God. They had seen Moses' face, still shining with the Glory of Heaven, with such a brightness, that it terrified them, and they had begged him to cover it, lest they be blinded by its brilliance, for he had been with God, and now he looked like God.

Theirs had been the generation that had such stories of miracles as never man had heard before: Water from a Rock that followed them in the wilderness, no matter where they went, angel's bread that dropped from the skies every morning, a mysterious Cloud that led them in their journeys, and a Pillar of Fire that covered, protected and kept them warm through the bitterly cold winter nights, keeping their "climate" moderate at all times. (I have slept at the foot of Mount Sinai in January, and I can testify that it was so cold, that I couldn't get warm all night, even though I was using a sub-zero sleeping bag).

But that generation was all gone, and this new generation, who had heard these stories, was beginning to doubt them and wonder if they weren't just a part of an imaginary, mythological past.

It is true that they still had a place where they could gather to worship, called the Tabernacle. It was at Shiloh. And men, who claimed to be descendants of the once great Aaron, the first High Priest, were still officiating in ceremonies that now seemed empty and without purpose. There was no partying and celebrating like the nations around them. But the sad fact is that during this time of great hardship their priests and prophets were silent. There was no prophetic Word of the Lord coming from their House of the Lord at Shiloh. Where were the "Defenders of the Faith" when the platform was set for greatness in man to emerge?

Why are the spiritual leaders so often significantly silent when it is time for great men to stand up and be counted? Is the clergy afraid to stand for truth because it might cost them a price? Did God have to use a woman under a palm tree because He couldn't find a man in His Holy Tabernacle?

Their pagan neighbours, whom they had failed to drive out, were getting stronger all the time, and even friendly towards them, inviting them to their pagan festivals which enticed the soul, as they filled the air with the sounds of a strange music they had never heard before. The brilliancy of colour was everywhere; the women were free and seemed so much happier. Besides, they had miracles too; their "gods" did strange and wondrous things for them, while their own God seemed farther and farther away; and the more they went after the strange gods the farther He seemed to withdraw from their presence. It wasn't hard to lose Him in the midst of their problems and the enticements of the world around them. Besides, it had become the acceptable thing to be "broad-minded" and accept other people's culture as being equal to their own.

Now and then a prophet of their faith passed through the land warning them, and some listened, and feared, and went to visit the Tabernacle at Shiloh to offer sacrifices; but for the most part, nobody paid much heed to these offensive old men who made them uncomfortable. This was a generation that, not only was forsaking their God, but was also forgetting the great Truths that He had given them in the Book of the Law. No one read it anymore. It was too restricting. Besides, if they read it they might get convicted by the Words that were written in it, which clearly showed them how far they had drifted from the Truths that were written in it.

This was a generation which *"knew not the Lord, nor yet the works which he had done for Israel."* And, what is worse the Book that tells their history records the terrible facts that they *"did evil in the sight of the Lord, and served Baalim: And they forsook the Lord God of their fathers, which brought them out of the land of Egypt, and followed other gods, of the gods of the people that were round about them, and bowed themselves unto them, and provoked the LORD to anger. And they forsook the LORD, and served Baal and Ashtaroth"* (Judges 2:10-13).

As a result of their sins and rejection of God, the warnings that the Lord had given long ago through Moses came upon them; their land was invaded by the very enemies of God with whom they had "flirted." They forsook God, and now He forsook them. The land was devoid of spiritual authority, and the people were without unity as *"every man did that which was right in his own eyes"* (Judges 17:6).

CALAMITY AND SUFFERING CAUSE PEOPLE TO TURN TO GOD

Those were barbaric times. As a result of these invasions by enemy nations, who occupied their land, there was great suffering in Israel. Their homes were raided and ransacked, their crops plundered, their maidens raped, their fathers mocked and their sons murdered. People could not walk the highways any more. There was great fear in the hearts of the people. They were locked up in their homes, and some even had to forsake their lands and dwellings because the enemy took possession of them. They lived in caves and dens. Their sheep and goats were stolen from them, their harvests were carried off as soon as they were reaped.

They lost their olives, their dates, their figs, their grapes, their wheat, their barley, and their pomegranates. This left them hungry, destitute, and desperate. The times were turbulent, living was one long trial, the faith of the few righteous was tested to its limit.

It is strange how, when people are suffering, they wonder where God is. But before that, they don't want Him. They throw Him out of their schools, their laws, the walls of their buildings, their hearts, and their lives. They say they don't need Him. They even make it a crime to pray to Him in public. But, when they are in trouble, they wonder where He is, and why He didn't save them and prevent tragedy!

During World War II when things were going badly for our troops in the front lines, the leaders of our nation always called us to pray. This was true during the first Gulf War crisis. America turned to God. When the tragic act of terror took place on September 11, 2001, and the World Trade Center was destroyed, with the terrible loss of many lives, and the Pentagon was badly damaged, it is significant how our country united together to pray and ask God for mercy!

Over and over again we read in the Bible, and in the history of the world, that when nations forgot and forsook the true God they had to suffer for it, but when they repented God was merciful and forgave them.

But, some leaders are too proud, or too wicked, to call for help from God, and ask their people to pray. I lived during the time of World War II, but I cannot remember Hitler ever calling for the people of Germany to pray; instead he told his Propaganda Minister, Paul Joseph Goebbels, to fill the ears of the German people with false reports of Germany's victories on their front lines. He was called a master of the "big lie." He directed his most vicious propaganda against the JEWS. He had complete control over the German radio, press, cinema and theater, and finally regimented all German culture. He ended his life by killing himself and his family in Hitler's bunker after Germany's defeat.

President Abraham Lincoln was a great man because he was not too proud to call for prayer.

I will never forget how we, in Canada, were called by our leaders to A Day of Prayer throughout Canada when 300,000 of our Allied troops made an unsuccessful attempt to land at Dunkirk, France, but were cut off by the Germans. The death toll would have been much greater if God had not supernaturally intervened. Many were rescued there by British ships and boats. Every man who owned a boat of any size was out on the English Channel, doing his duty for God and Country. Oh, how brave our men were! And the women who stood behind their men were brave too.

THE WICKED JABIN, THE KING OF CANAAN

Among the nations that occupied Israel, none were more cruel than the Canaanites, under their powerful and evil King Jabin.

Almost a century before that, his predecessor, whose name was also Jabin, King of Hazor, had convinced four other kings to make a confederation of evil against Israel. But Joshua destroyed the city of Hazor, burned it to the ground, killed Jabin with the edge of the sword, and defeated his evil axis, scattering them back to Tyrus in the West, and Mizpeh, in the East.

Hazor's royal family apparently fled to a place called Harosheth of the Gentiles. Now, out of the ashes of the burnt and destroyed city of Hazor there rose up this son of the pagan gods who seemed to be a "reincarnation" of an earlier King Jabin whom Joshua had defeated, and killed with the sword (Joshua 11:1-14). He was filled with bitterness and revenge over the defeats his ancestors had experienced in the past, and now, with his powerful general, Sisera, who was a resident of Jabin's city of refuge, he marched against the Israelites and occupied their land. The Book of Judges tells us that he "mightily oppressed" the Children of Israel for twenty long years (Judges 4:3).

It is interesting that the name "Harosheth" means "Smithy." Alfred Eldersheim says it was "probably so called from being the arsenal where his iron war-chariots, armed with scythes, were made." He believes that the site of this place is somewhere in the neighborhood of Bethshean, which afterwards formed the southernmost point of Galilee. He says it was south of Mount Tabor.

King Jabin's strength lay in his powerful army. The historian, Josephus writes that under the command of his general, Sisera, he had 300,000 footmen, 10,000 horsemen, and 900 hundred chariots of iron. These chariots, not only controlled the highways and roads of the land, they could be driven through an army of men, and with the swords in their wheels they could cut off the legs of the strongest and bravest of soldiers. They were feared, as tanks are today. The people of Israel had no answer to such deadly weapons of mass destruction, forged in the bowels of hell. The men trembled at the very thought of these dreadful machines slicing into their armies—this is supposing there was an army willing to go up against Jabin; but no one would volunteer, terrified of challenging such a formidable foe. The bravest of them were in hiding, together with their women and children.

That is when Israel began to call upon the Lord for help. They came to visit the Prophetess Deborah, telling her about their troubles and their suffering. Asking for prayer and guidance as to what they should do to save their lives, and the lives of their families.

Why does it take a national calamity to bring a nation back to God? It is a sad fact that great suffering causes people to turn to God. That is what Israel did. The Bible says, *"The Children of Israel cried unto the Lord"* (Judges 4:3).

Tribulation turns a nation back to God. It drives people to their knees. Man's utter hopelessness causes him to turn to God for help. What will it take to turn the nations of our day back to God? Will it take the wrath of evil men, dictators, monsters, men without mercy to drive this generation to the Seat of Mercy, and into the arms of a Merciful God?

That is what happened in the days of the Judges. In the midst of all their tribulation and reign of terror God quietly and secretly raised up a leader from among the people, a judge superior to all the judges before her, and most of those who came after her, because she was not only a judge (ruler), she was a prophetess and a woman who possessed military intelligence. She had the prophetic insight for her people. Only Samuel had a gift of prophecy that equaled hers. But when she later spoke about herself she called herself "A mother in Israel." She loved her people, she prayed for them, pitied them, reproved them, and risked her life for them when she marched as a general with Barak in one of Israel's greatest battles. She was fearless, and she was great in the eyes of God and the hearts of her people. Her love and her wisdom had made her great. There is no record of her having given birth to any children; but her people, all the children of Israel, were her children. A great leader always makes great sacrifices for those whom God puts under her care.

Indira Gandhi, the great Prime Minister of India, (1966-1977) was once asked if she would ever marry again (she had been divorced many years earlier). She answered, "Never! My heart belongs to my people!"

Queen Elizabeth I, who was one of England's greatest monarchs refused to marry because she wanted to devote her whole heart and life to her people.

WHY DID GOD CHOOSE A WOMAN?

Through the years many men have asked, "Why did God choose a woman? Why didn't He choose a man as His prophet in those perilous times?" I believe it was for two reasons. One: God can choose whomsoever He wills. Two: Because Deborah was a woman the enemy would never suspect how great a threat she was to his evil schemes. He did not dream that a woman would lead the people, whom he kept in oppressive enslavement, in a *"War of Liberation."* Women have great advantage over men, because no one believes what great things they are capable of doing; by the time they wake up, its too late. (He chooses the foolish things to confound the wise). Someone has said that women are God's secret weapons!

The place where she lived is close to the proximity where another Deborah was buried, the nurse of Rebekah who had died and was buried under a great Oak Tree (Genesis 35:8). It was here, at Bethel, that Jacob had met with God as he fled from his brother, Esau. Here, in a dream, the Lord had shown him a ladder that reached from earth to Heaven, which caused him to call the place "Bethel" (The House of God). Much later, on his return to the Land from Mesopotamia, Jacob and his family had a very important meeting with God. They got rid of all their idols, and made a fresh dedication of their lives to Him. After all these years, Bethel was still "The House of God" and the Presence of God was still there. God still met with His people there and spoke to them. Certain places on earth are anointed of God. And even after many years, one can still feel the Presence of God there. So it is at the Western Wall in Jerusalem.

The Bible says that the first Deborah, the nurse of Rebekah, was buried under an Oak Tree (Genesis 35:8). This Deborah dwelt under a palm tree. Palm trees are known for their deep roots. They can survive strong storms which would uproot, break or destroy even strong oaks. A palm tree's strength lies in its roots and its flexibility to bend with the forces of the storm.

A great leader must have these qualifications. Opposition will never have the power to uproot those whose convictions are anchored because they have an inner strength that is hidden to the world. A great leader will also have the ability to appear to yield under pressure, but will actually bounce right back up when things calm down again.

Such a person was Deborah, our prophetess. She had the ability to survive the storms that threatened her people from the wicked Canaanites in Northern Galilee. It is believed, by many scholars, that she was a daughter of the Tribe of Issachar. This made it twice as hard for her to endure steadfastly in her calling, because it was in this tribal area that the enemy had firmly entrenched himself and overtaken the land. He was on every hand. He was always watching, spying, and getting people in trouble. But his presence did not daunt her, because the Presence of the Lord was like a bubble around her. She had her own personal "Cloud by day, and pillar of fire by night" She lived in the *Shekinah* of the *Ruach Ha Kodesh.* That is why she was titled, "The Woman of Light."

I have met these "daughters of light" in some of the most unexpected places. If I told you, you wouldn't believe me. So why don't you ask the Lord to help you find your own? Don't think that they are all in your religious environment. Some haven't ever been inside a church. But you can see Jesus in their eyes.

Israel knew that Deborah was "a woman sent from God." They knew this about John the Baptist too (John 1:6). Just because the religious leaders of his day did not recognize nor accept him, did not disqualify him from his high calling. John had the authority of Heaven, and Deborah did too. They were both qualified to speak in the name of God.

DEBORAH PRAYS THROUGH

No one knew the hearts of the people better than Deborah. As they came to her with their pains, their sorrows, their broken hearts and the burden of their transgressions and guilt, they would confess their sins to her. She knew the heart of Israel, and, as a true mother in Israel, she became an intercessor for her people. There were many nights when, after a long day of comforting, exhorting, correcting and praying for her people, she would weep in the darkness of the night for God to have mercy on Israel, and send deliverance.

No one is as qualified to carry the responsibility of government as the one who has wept and prayed through to victory at the Throne Room of Heaven! Day after day she saw and heard about the wretched state of the people as they showed her their wounds and the terrible scars of their beatings. Fathers told how their wives and young daughters had been shamefully and viciously abused, their sons tortured and killed in front of their eyes, and many other things too cruel to write about. This happened year after year for twenty long years; and as time went by things only continued to worsen under the oppressive cruelty of King Jabin; until finally "his cup of iniquity was full."

This time, when Israel cried out to God in desperation for Divine Intervention, God said, "Enough!"

He spoke to Deborah and told her to send for Barak, the son of Abinoam, who was living in Kedesh-Naphtali (about four miles from the north end of the "waters of Meroth").

DEBORAH IS COMMANDED OF GOD TO SEND FOR BARAK

When Barak was told that Deborah was calling for him to come, he immediately knew in his heart that this was not a call from a woman, it was a call from Ha Shem!

His heart was racing as he travelled by foot from the Tribe of Naphtali to the territory of the Tribe of Issachar, the very heart of enemy occupation. Most of us would have sent excuses! But he hurried to the place of the Palm Tree where the great "Mother in Israel" spoke the oracles of God to her people.

When he stood before her, she did not *command* him, she *asked* him if he had heard God speak to his heart, "*Hath not the LORD God of Israel commanded, saying, Go and draw toward mount Tabor, and take with thee ten thousand men of the children of Naphtali and of the children of Zebulun?*" (Judges 4:6)

Most of the time, when we receive a prophecy through someone, it is a confirmation of something that the Lord has already spoken to us. When that happens it is time to sit up and take notice.

Deborah knew that God had spoken to him, and had even told him how to "fix" the battle. That is one of the wonderful things about the gift of prophecy; it is usually a confirmation of something that God has already spoken. It is a confirmation of what the heart already knows. And Deborah knew that God had already called Barak to the battle so he just needed this extra "prophetic shove."

As she looked at this young, handsome son of the Tribe of Naphtali standing before her, she didn't just see him on the outside, she could see right into his heart. She knew the call of God that was on his life. It wasn't her call! It was God's call that had brought him into her presence. She knew what the Lord had spoken to him before he ever arrived. It was as though she had heard all that God had said to him, and how He had dealt with his heart. Let us go with Deborah into the background which is not recorded in our Bible.

I too can picture Barak, that son of the Tribe of Naphtali, as he sits, hiding in his den or cave, and God is speaking to him, telling him that he has been chosen to lead the Children of Israel to battle against their powerful enemy, the destroyer of their land and their lives.

Barak considers his youth, his inexperience, and his empty hands, and thinks that he must be crazy to imagine that he could do anything to save Israel from so powerful an enemy. He shakes his head, and says to himself, "How could I tell anyone that God has chosen me to raise up an army to liberate us from our bondage? No one would ever believe me. It is impossible! I must be crazy! Besides, we haven't even one single weapon of any kind in all of Israel. I haven't seen a shield or spear in Israel. We are defenseless."

THE CALL OF GOD CONFIRMED

How many of us have a hard time believing that God can use us in a great way! We feel so small and useless. But we must take our eyes off ourselves, and put them on the Lord. It is not our strength, nor our talents that will save the day, it is the almighty power of an Almighty God. Barak was just the "suit of armour" that God wore when He went to battle against His enemy who had blasphemed Him and enticed His people to worship false gods. Every battle in our lives is God's battle; He just lets us have the honour of getting the credit for it.

Now, as Barak stands there, looking at this Mother in Israel, he shifts his legs uneasily because he knows she is "reading his mail."

"Barak, son of Abinoam," she begins, "hasn't the Lord God Jehovah of Israel commanded you what He wants you to do?"

It seemed to him as though her eyes pierced through to his soul. He couldn't deny it.

Then she began to give him military instruction for warfare and prophesy what the results would be, "*Go and draw toward Mount Tabor, and take with thee ten thousand men of the children of Naphtali and of the children of Zebulun? And I Jehovah will draw unto thee to the river Kishon Sisera, the captain of Jabin's army Sisera, with his chariots and his multitude; and I will deliver him into thine hand* (Judges 4:6b-7).

As he hears this prophetess tell him the secrets of God which he had kept hidden in his heart, he knew it was a confirmation of what he had felt, but had told no one. I can imagine how shaken he was when Deborah looked him straight in the eye, and told him the thing he was hoping was only a foolish notion was the call of God upon his life. He thought, "This is too big a responsibility for me. I am not qualified for the task. God needs some great champion, a 'lion' of Judah, not a Naphtalite!"

Not only did she know that Ha Shem had called Barak to lead His people to the War of Liberation, she saw, by the Spirit, the military strategy that God wanted him to use.

There is no doubt that the reason Israel has almost never lost a battle in all its history is because they get their military intelligence from a higher "Military Pentagon" than the one in Washington, D.C. His war plans can never fail. The Commander-in-Chief of this army never makes a mistake. God fights the battles of Israel; and He knows how to fight His own battles.

King Jabin's soldiers were scattered throughout the region, but God promised that He would draw them out to the River Kishon, where they would expose themselves, and that when God got them all together in one place, He Himself, would hand them over into the hands of Israel under the command of His General, Barak. What a sure and positive promise of victory!

OUR HESITATION GRIEVES THE HOLY SPIRIT

But in spite of such wonderful promises of a sure victory, Barak hesitated. He really didn't want the job. He had no desire to be a soldier, let alone, be the great heroic commander of ten thousand soldiers in any army, even the Lord's!

Many have criticized Barak because of his doubts and fears, but when you understand that he belonged to the Tribe of Naphtali you know why he was like that. The Tribe of Naphtali are NOT "fighters." A Naphtalite avoids confrontation, if at all possible. Right then, he would rather have escaped out of his situation, leaped over a wall, and skipped about on some distant mountaintop as far from there as possible. But he was a captive of a powerful God and His prophetess, and there was no way he could get out of it, no place to hide.

Suddenly he got the idea, he would go to battle on the one condition, that Deborah would go with him. Surely she would refuse, after all, she was a woman, and she was therefore not strong enough for battle. Besides, she was getting on in years and she had her important ministry of taking care of the crowds who came to see her every day, so he challenged her, *"If thou wilt go with me, then I will go: but if thou wilt not go with me, then I will not go"* (Judges 4:8).

His answer grieved the Holy Spirit because it revealed his lack of trust and faith in the anointed prophetic word. It also revealed that he had more faith in a human being than in the Lord, Himself.

Deborah too was grieved in her spirit, because she wanted to see a more willing response. Women hate cowardice in men. How sad it makes us feel when we see men are more afraid of standing up against the enemy than we are! Women want to see men as being men of strength and courage. It is so important that the leader of the army is full of faith, otherwise, there is no way that the men following him can have faith. The Lord said to Joshua, *"Have not I commanded thee?*

Be strong and of a good courage; be not afraid, neither be thou dismayed: for the LORD thy God is with thee whithersoever thou goest" (Joshua 1:9).

Nevertheless Deborah rose up and went along with Barak when he returned to his home base, Kedesh-Naphtali where he was to summon the tribes of Zebulun and Naphtali to battle.

Amazingly, God not only chose a Naphtalite as His commander, the troops whom the Lord had conscripted for the battle were from the tribes of Naphtali and Zebulun, who also were not born fighters. This was one war where God was choosing the most unlikely Tribes to do warfare.

You may not be a born "fighter" either. So you better beware, it is quite probable that the Lord will choose you so that He can get the honour of winning the victory. Does the Word not say, *"The race is not to the swift, nor the battle to the strong, neither yet bread to the wise, nor yet riches to men of understanding, nor yet favour to men of skill; but time and chance happeneth to them all"* (Ecclesiastes 9:11)?

WILL SOMEONE ELSE GET THE HONOURS THAT COULD HAVE BEEN YOURS?

Barak found out that no matter how he felt, God had chosen His champion who would destroy the foe; the only trouble was that His champion didn't believe either he or God could do it. God's help wasn't enough; he needed a woman to go with him! He needed a woman of faith. Who had more faith than the prophetess of the Lord?

Deborah had faith in her own prophecy, she knew they would win the battle. She answered Barak, "*I will surely go with thee: notwithstanding the journey that thou takest shall not be for thine honour; for the LORD shall sell Sisera into the hand of a woman*" (Judges 4:9)

How sad! The first promise was that God would deliver Sisera, the captain of Jabin's army with his chariots and his multitude into Barak's hand. Now, because he had lacked in faith and courage God said that the journey that he would take would not be for his honour, God would deliver Captain Sisera into the hand of a woman.

Josephus, in writing *Antiquities of the Jews,* relates that Deborah said, "Thou, O Barak, deliverest up meanly ignobly that authority which God hath given thee into the hand of a woman, and I do not reject it!"

I wonder how many honours we lose in life because we hesitate. Someone once said "He who hesitates is lost." We may not lose our souls, but we still can suffer the loss of great honours and rewards when we come to the end of our lives.

Jewish history tells us that when the men of Israel feared to enter the Promised Land, in the days of Joshua and Caleb, that the women were not a part of their rebellion. In the book, *To Be A Jewish Woman* we read on page 58, "The Jewish women in the desert did not listen to the spies' report. They wanted to go into The Promised Land. Due to their righteousness, they did not die in the desert, as did their male contemporaries. Due to their love of the land, the women all entered the land of Israel under the leadership of Joshua. Through the women's demonstration of their love of God in these matters, they showed themselves to be in tune with His will. Their behaviour was so exemplary that had the men acted as the women did, the Messiah would have come during the time of the desert generation."

The author goes on to say that Deborah was the greatest Jew of her generation (the *gaddol ha-dor*), and she lived during the time when judges ruled the Jewish people. Since no men of her era were qualified to be judges, the entire Jewish nation came to her to be judged."

God will choose whom He will. If we rebel against the one whom He chooses, male or female, we are rebelling against the Lord.

Someone once asked Kathryn Kuhlman why she was preaching the Gospel and healing the sick, when she was a woman. She answered, "Because the man God called wouldn't go!"

I wonder how many men have refused the calling to be the General of the Lord's army in the nations of the world, because they counted it as a profession beneath them. And because they refused to surrender their lives to the Lord, God called "a woman" who heard the call and answered, "I do not reject it!"

So it was that Deborah went along with Barak when he returned to Kedesh-Naphtali, where he had been commanded to call the two Tribes of Naphtali and Zebulun to assemble.

What are you doing with your life, dear reader? Is this "journey of life" which you are making going to be one that will end without honour? Think it over carefully! Are you doing God's will? Are you fulfilling your life's calling? When your life is over will you have finished your course? Will you find a crown of righteousness waiting for you?

Apostle Paul, at the end of his life, wrote to his spiritual son from a Roman prison, "*I have fought a good fight, I have finished my course, I have kept the faith: Henceforth there is laid up for me a crown of righteousness, which the Lord, the righteous judge, shall give me at that day: and not to me only, but unto all them also that love his appearing*" (2 Timothy 4:7-8). Will you be able to say the same in the last days of your earthly life?

WHY DID GOD CHOOSE THE TRIBES OF NAPHTALI AND ZEBULUN?

Of the twelve tribes of Israel, Naphtali and Zebulun were the least gifted for warfare. They could fight if they had to, but they much preferred avoiding any kind of trouble. Naphtali was *"a hind* [a female deer] *let loose"* (Genesis 49:21). "She" was a free-spirited tribe. She wanted to be left to herself, do her own thing, live her own life. She hated rules and regulations. She was not created to obey commands of any kind.

As for Zebulun, it was the tribe that dwelt by the sea (Genesis 49:13), and loved nothing more than swimming and fishing, or going out to sea. It hated trouble of any kind, and avoided confrontation if at all possible. It would just as soon sail out to sea in stormy weather as face an enemy. Both tribes were easy to live with, got along with people, and neither of them were trouble makers in any way. Naphtali loved her mountains, and Zebulun loved his sea. Naphtali's feet were sure on the highest and steepest of cliffs, and Zebulun's were happiest in the soft rocking of the boat as it launched out to yon distant isle.

Judah was the warring tribe. Why didn't God choose Judah, or Gad, (who always loves a fight), or Dan, who goes looking for some new land to conquer; a man from his tribe was capable of killing a thousand men with the "jawbone of an ass." And what about Ephraim, the great warriors of Israel, and Manasseh, who stood his ground and remained unmovable under the most violent circumstances? Even little Benjamin was a frisky fighter — anyone — but not Zebulun and Naphtali!

Again, God chooses whom He will. It wasn't the men, who were untrained for warfare, who would win the battle; it was the Lord. If He could win the battle with three hundred men and one Gideon (a man of the tribe of Manasseh), He could surely win the battle through 10,000 Zebulunites and Naphtalites — even though the enemy (according to Historian Josephus) had 300,000 footmen, 10,000 cavalry and 900 chariots of iron! The important thing to know when you go to battle, is not who has the strongest army, but whose side God is on!

In two World Wars the German army issued buckles for their soldiers' belts with the slogan, *"Gott mit uns."* (God with us), but in the end it was only a slogan. In the end, Germany lost both wars. He was with the Allies who defeated the powerful German army.

WHAT HAD HAPPENED TO THE OTHERS? WHERE WERE THEY?

In a patriarchal society it was a sign and a wonder that the Lord placed a woman in such a powerful and important position of authority. Deborah's fame spread abroad throughout the land, and as many as were able, came "for judgment." Her word was final. No one doubted it. They went away knowing they had heard from God.

This was not a new thing in the world. In Greece, the people would come to Delphi to hear a woman, who was called the "Oracle," give them "the word of the gods." But in Israel it was a new thing for a woman to be the prophetic judge of the land.

Seeing the people had faith in her, why then, didn't all the tribes volunteer to go to war? Was it because Deborah only mentioned Naphtali and Zebulun? Why did God choose these two to lead in the battle?

God knew what He would do, and that the battle would be won. He even knew how it would be won. He knew that the battle would last but a day, and it was no use calling all the men from all of Israel to a battle that was already fought and won in the plan of Heaven.

Nevertheless, in her “Song of Victory” Deborah rebukes the Tribes who did not volunteer. Why didn’t they want to have the opportunity to participate in this great victory? Apparently some of them did join in before the battle was over. What about the others? Surely they knew all about it. News travels fast — especially bad news! They knew that Israel was fighting for her life, her very existence.

Zebulon and Naphtali were conscripted by the Lord. But some of the other Tribes volunteered. Who were they? Let us look at them.

1. **EPHRAIM**: (Judges 5:14a) *“Out of Ephraim was there a root of them against Amalek.”* Apparently there were not very many of them who came, but those who did were the experienced warriors, the old veterans of past battles who were the root of the tribe. God always has His old soldiers who never want to miss a battle. They are the kind who will “die with their boots on.”

2. **BENJAMIN:** (Judges 5.14b) *"After thee, Benjamin, among thy people;"* The tribe of Benjamin was the smallest of the tribes. They lived down around Jerusalem. They had to travel a long way by foot, but they too were ready fighters, and with the first sound of the trumpet they were off to battle.

3. **MANASSEH:** (Judges 5:14c) *"Out of Machir came down governors."* These were the "princes" of the great old families of Manasseh. They were the steady, reliable fathers of the faith, who still had some of that "old time religion" in them. It would be one of their sons, Gideon, who would become the next judge.

4. **ZEBULUN**: (Judges 5:14d) "*...and out of Zebulun they that handle the pen of the writer.*" Besides loving her sea-life, Zebulun is a gifted writer. The anointing to write prose and poetry is a gift that inspires every Zebulunite.

5. **ISSACHAR:** (Judges 5:15a) *"And the princes of Issachar were with Deborah; even Issachar, and also Barak: he was sent on foot into the valley."* For Issachar to venture forth into battle took great courage because most

of their area was under the control of the powerful enemy. There were eyes everywhere that would see when anyone made a move. But they were strong men who had understanding concerning the times in which they were living (1 Chronicles 12:32); and even though God had not required them to make this supreme sacrifice, they volunteered to fight the battle of the Lord. The courage of one man or woman to volunteer for the army of the Lord always inspires other men and women. Most of Issachar's territory lay in the valley where this battle took place.

When we add to these four, Zebulun and Naphtali, we have six Tribes that joined in solidarity with the Lord's call for the deliverance of Israel from her enemies. Six out of twelve! Why do people always have to be divided, even when the cause is a righteous one, and for the benefit of their own country?

Now, let us look at the Tribes that Deborah and Barak rebuked when they sang their famous **Hymn of Victory.**

1. **REUBEN**: (Judges 5:15b-16) *"For the divisions of Reuben there were great*

searchings of heart. Why abodest thou among the sheepfolds, to hear the bleatings of the flocks? For the divisions of Reuben there were great searchings of heart." There was a lot of talk, discussion and arguing going on, but no one was willing to get involved personally in this life-and-death battle for the survival of their nation and their brethren. It sounds much like the United Nations of today! Besides, the Tribe of Reuben still had their great flocks and herds, like they had when they chose the eastern side of the Jordan for their inheritance. They would rather sit in the green pastures with their sheep and goats, listening to the piping of the shepherd as he played his sweet melody in the peaceful surroundings of a land that was far away from the battlefield.

2. **GAD**: (Judges 5:17a) *"Gilead abode beyond Jordan:"* Gilead was the land of Gad which was also situated on the East side of the Jordan River. They thought they were safe from King Jabin, so why get involved?

3. **DAN**: (Judges 5:17b) *"And why did Dan remain in ships?"* Part of the Tribe of Dan dwelt on the southern coasts of the land. They had become a sea-going tribe.

Now they were involved in the import-export business. They were busy making money. They would rather stay home and "buy war-bonds" so that they could have a clear conscience because of their "effort." Let others go to battle and lose their lives. Israel needed her financiers. That was the role they would play!

4. **ASHER**: (Judges 5:17) *"Asher sat at the shore by the water, and remained by his havens."* (*Hendrickson Interlinear Bible*). Asher is the Tribe that enjoys nothing more than to lie on the beach and watch the water, taking an occasional dip in its crystal blue coolness. Who wants to go to battle, when he can sit by the sea shore, digging in the sand with his toes, and making sand castles?

Three tribes are not even mentioned: **Judah, Simeon, and Levi.**

We can understand why Levi was not mentioned. They were the priestly tribe. They had no inheritance in the land of Israel. They dwelt in cities that were scattered throughout the nation. They were not expected to go to battle.

But what about Judah, the Lion of the Tribes? Was he too busy with his own projects, schemes and dreams to come? And was Simeon deaf to the call of God, Simeon, who is known as the Tribe that can hear the voice of God? How quickly we can backslide from our callings and our anointings! We must all take heed, lest we fall. There is no guarantee that we will possess the greatness of God that we possessed yesterday when we face the great trials of tomorrow. We need to walk very carefully before God, lest we find ourselves missing when the *Honour Roll* is called, as it is in these two chapters in Judges.

The shining example of the warriors is a big contrast to the cowardice and indifference of the ones who shirked their country's call to serve in the day of battle.

On the Honour Roll two Tribes shine out, Zebulun and Naphtali. They get the Highest Medal of Honour for deeds of exceptional valour. *"Zebulun and Naphtali were a people that jeoparded their lives unto the death in the high places of the field"* (Judges 5:18). They feared not to march into the face of the most powerful, mightily-equipped army of their time, and stand their ground in the heat of the toughest battle. Israel still has soldiers like that today.

BARAK MARTIALS THE TROOPS

Once Barak had Deborah's promise he called out the troops. He did everything according to the plan. His problem wasn't that he was rebellious, it was just that he didn't want to be involved in any battles. God has a lot of people like that. But in these last days we will have to make up our minds that life is going to be one long battle from here on out, and we might as well put on the full armour of God so that we can stand and fight against the wiles of the devil. There is no place for "peaceniks" in these last days.

Never look at your own weakness, or your own lack of military experience and knowledge. Keep your eyes on the Captain of the Hosts of Heaven. He will lead you through every battle, and bring you out more than a conqueror. God is a "winner" and when He fights your battle you are a "winner" too. He still can kill a "Goliath" with one smooth stone! But it takes a brave and courageous David to face the enemy in the *"name of the Lord of hosts, the God of the armies of Israel"* (1 Samuel 17:45).

When David defied the giant Goliath he was without fear. This was because David knew his God. When you know the greatness of God it takes all fear out of your heart.

As the troops gathered together on foot from throughout their regions, they came as they were, in their humble farmer's clothing, most of which was ragged because of their poverty. No one was wearing a uniform, and few, if any, had weapons, for Judges 5:8 said that among as many as 40,000 men in Israel there couldn't be found one single spear or sword. The enemy had confiscated all these long before. No wonder God didn't need more than 10,000 men! He wasn't going to use men to win the battle anyway. Nor was he going to use military equipment. He would use the weather—the hail and the wind and the powerful rain. He would turn the Wadi Kishon into a torrential river that overflowed its banks, for it is "*Not by might, nor by power, but by my spirit, saith the LORD of hosts*" (Zechariah 4:6).

Deborah was not wrong when she said that God only needed ten thousand to put to death the mighty hosts. Barak's men were the Lord's servants whom He used to turn the fields of the Jezreel Valley into a Valley of Blood. This was the first great battle to be fought on the plains of the future Armageddon, but it wasn't the last. The last and final battle when the blood will flow to the horse's bridle is still to be fought, and it is not far off. But we know who will win! And we know that even as God used Deborah to lead the army of the Lord to victory then, He again is using His prophetesses in these last days to speak forth the Word of God to the troops of the Lord, with the promise of victory. I am wondering, will the Lord "sell the enemy into the hands of a woman again?" Will women have a very prominent leadership role to play in the end-time army? I believe they will!

The call-up for Barak's army was not advertised on the billboards of Israel. It was done in secret. Men whispered the call into the ears of their brothers, their cousins, and their closest friends. Only those who could be trusted could be told to present themselves at Kedesh-Naphtali as volunteers for the army.

Secrecy is not always a sign of cowardice. It is wise military strategy, when one is fighting a powerful enemy.

We must learn to understand that there are times when "keeping God's secret" is not cowardly nor deceitful. Proverbs 25:2 says, *"It is the glory of God to conceal a thing:"*

In the darkness of the night men started kissing their mothers and their wives goodbye, comforting them, "Don't be afraid; I will return. This is the Lord's battle." After whispering a prayer to Ha Shem, they quietly slipped away under the cover of darkness. While the enemy slept, brave men of Israel were gathering together at Kedesh-Naphtali. And angels were arriving from Heaven and all over the world to help them. They were not alone.

When you go to war, remember that you are never alone. The warring angels are at your side twenty-four hours a day.

When the ten thousand had been assembled, they moved to Mount Tabor, where they pitched their camp.

EVIL MEN INFORM KING JABIN THAT THERE IS SUSPICIOUS MOVEMENT IN ISRAEL

There was a certain clan living in Israel at that time who were not Israelites, nor

Canaanites. They were Kenites. This clan was fathered by a man called Heber. Heber was a descendent of Moses' father-in-law, Jethro. Heber, no doubt to make his life under the occupation more comfortable and advantageous, had become friendly with Israel's enemy, King Jabin. There was something treacherous and conniving about Heber. He had separated himself from the rest of his people. He had a rebellious spirit. He was the type of man whom no one could trust. His motives were evil, for he would betray others in the interests of self-promotion. He had pitched his tent in the vicinity of Kedesh, of Naphtali, the area where Barak lived, and where the Lord had told him to gather the troops.

It didn't take long before Heber discovered what was happening, and immediately he sent informants to King Jabin (Judges 4:11-12). But this was all a part of the Lord's military strategy, for while King Jabin rallied to mobilize his great army the Lord was preparing His Heavenly hosts to "meet him in the way."

When King Jabin heard that Israel was preparing to rise up against him he was filled with rage. How dare those Israelites try to revolt against him! He would crush them with his powerful army. He commanded his general, Sisera, to go and destroy those "rebels."

Within days Sisera had martialed his troops and they have marched by the thousands from all directions to Mount Tabor where they pitched their camp not far from Barak's army.

Josephus says that when Barak and his soldiers saw the great multitude that they were so afraid that they resolved to march off, had not Deborah restrained them, and commanded them to fight the enemy that very day, for that was the day they would conquer them, and God would be their assistance.

The Bible tells the story in a very soul-stirring way, *"And Deborah said unto Barak, Up; for this is the day in which the LORD hath delivered Sisera into thine hand: is not the LORD gone out before thee? So Barak went down from mount Tabor, and ten thousand men after him"* (Judges 4:14).

It is awesome to know that the day which we fear the most can be the day of our greatest victory. When all hell is arrayed against you, don't run away.

Apostle James writes, "*Submit yourselves therefore to God. Resist the devil, and he will flee from you*" (James 4:7).

When you are submissive to the will of God, you are powerful in Him. Obedience makes us strong, and puts the devil on the run. So, the best way to resist the devil is to be obedient to the will of God. The powers of darkness that you face will turn into the Glory of God.

Don't look at the size of the enemy. Keep your eyes on the Lord.

THE BLOODY BATTLE

"UP; FOR THIS IS THE DAY IN WHICH THE LORD HATH DELIVERED SISERA INTO THINE HAND: IS NOT THE LORD GONE OUT BEFORE THEE?"

The command to march, as it was shouted from the heart of Deborah was like the blast of the shofar! It echoed to the last man on the mount. And as its sound reached their ears, the power of God was in it. For the courage of a lion filled their spirits, and the strength of a mighty warrior came into the limbs of those young farmer-boys, who today would have come out of their *kibbutzim*. The Lord, seeing them charge down Mount Tabor, rose up from His throne and came down from Heaven, and led His own heavenly hosts to march before them. He, and His army would be the first to reach the enemy!

When the Lord sends you to the mission field, or into any difficult assignment, be it physical or spiritual, remember that He has gone out before you! He is the buffer between you and all of hell's opposing forces.

Suddenly, the sky was filled with dark, threatening clouds. Fear began to fill the hearts of the enemy, the terror of God gripped the hearts of the Canaanites. Their gods did not fight for them. They were no protection from this Almighty God of Israel Who was stirred up in great anger against them.

But they did not dare attempt to escape the confrontation, for their officers would have killed them; so they marched into the face of conflict and certain death. And as they did, great drops of rain began pelting from heaven. Soon it became a torrential downpour, turning the ground into mud and mire, causing their horses to sink down in it, and they, themselves, to lose their footing and fall. Then, as the heaven's darkened still more, the rain turned into hail, hail that was driven by strong, stormy winds into their faces, blinding them so that they couldn't even see who was their enemy, and who was their comrade in arms. The extreme cold, together with the hail, turned everything to ice so that their arrows and slings were of no advantage to them.

Their swords hung unused at their sides. The men became like frozen statues in full armour, armour that was useless for the battle. The roaring of the wind, together with the freezing cold, for which they were not prepared nor dressed, almost paralyzed them, and their commanders were unable to issue commands that could be heard. All communication was broken down.

The storm that was blowing into the faces of the soldiers of Sisera did not hinder

Israel because it was to their backs. The God of the Storms had not directed it against His army. When the Israelites saw what was happening they took courage, because they knew that God was helping them right before their eyes. Josephus writes, "They fell upon the very midst of their enemies and slew a great number of them; so that some of them fell by the Israelites, some fell by their own horses, which were put into disorder, and not a few were killed by their own chariots." The swords on the wheels of the chariots, which Israel had so greatly feared, cut off their own legs, leaving a bloody massacre of men screaming and dying in pain and anguish. Consternation ruled the day. Demons joined the screaming men, and angels roared in triumph. The plain of Jezreel was covered with blood.

Realizing that his army was thrown into a panic before the onslaught of Barak and his God; and that they were suffering humiliating defeat, Sisera, in his ultimate display of self-preservation, and in desperation, leaped from his chariot, and fled for his life, deserting his soldiers, and leaving them to die alone and confused.

That is what often happens when an evil despot rules. In the time of battle, when he sees that all hope of victory is lost, he vanishes. He escapes to let others face the fire while he hides in some remote, hiding place which he has prepared for himself long before the conflagration ever began.

Sisera turned and ran for his life. Now the wind was at his back, the hail and the rain no longer striking his face. He could see, and he knew the direction he must go to escape from it all.

And as he ran, he saw a nomadic tent in the distance. He recognizes it as The Tent of Heber, his friend. He had often sat in the king's house, drinking wine with Heber in the presence of King Jabin.

"Ach," he says to himself, "a place of refuge! I will stop for a moment and hide in the tent until the storm passes by, and then, under cover of darkness I will return to my mother who is waiting for me back home."

He never dreamed that he would never reach home, nor see his mother again. She would wait in vain, watching at the window, for her son's return with the plunder from the war.

JAEL

The story of Deborah and Barak's great victory would not be complete without telling about "that other woman" who played a very prominent and important part in Israel's victory over the Canaanites.

Jael was the wife of Heber, a Kenite. As already mentioned, he was a descendent of Jethro, the father-in-law of Moses. But he had broken ties with his tribe, and was living apart with his immediate family, near to where the battle took place.

Because of Heber's close alliance and friendship with King Jabin, Heber, no doubt enjoyed special privileges, such as not having to pay tribute to the Canaanites. The Bible says, *"Sisera fled away on his feet to the tent of Jael the wife of Heber the Kenite: for there was peace between Jabin the king of Hazor and the house of Heber the Kenite"* (Judges 4:17).

In that society the women often had their own tents to dwell in. By doing this, their husbands were able to entertain their male friends privately, without having women in their presence. It was very improper for any man, other than her husband, or son, or an immediate male family member to enter the tent of the women.

Why then, did Sisera run to Jael's tent? And where was her husband, Heber, on that important day? Was he in Hazor, giving advice to King Jabin, or had he even participated in the battle? No one knows. The Bible doesn't tell us. But we do know that Jael was all alone. Not even her children nor servants were there, and surely, considering they were people of such importance, they would have had servants! Had God arranged it so that she would be completely alone in that Middle East society? Only God could have made this possible!

Sometimes, when God has a very important assignment for us, and he knows that others would hinder us, He works things out so that there isn't a single person around who could interfere with us carrying out the plan of God.

I remember the first time the Lord called me to a twenty-one day fast. My husband, my children's father, was in the Philippines, but he was supposed to come home that day. I knew that if he did, I would not be able to fast. So I prayed for God to give me an "appointment to fast." Before the day was over he called me from the Philippines and told me that he would have to stay another three weeks in Manila. I had a hard time keeping myself from shouting "hallelujah" over the phone. I knew that the Lord had removed the hindrances. I was on my way to a "breakthrough." My life has never been the same since.

If you need a time alone with God, ask Him to "clean out the house." He can do it.

"TURN IN, MY LORD!"

Jael must have had a premonition of something special going to happen that day because she was apparently waiting for Sisera. She saw him, as he came running in her direction, and she "went out to meet him" and said to him, "Turn in, my lord, turn in to me; fear not."

I suspect that she hated Sisera. Perhaps, during some of the times when he had visited Heber, she had listened to their conversation, and had discovered the evil that was in that man's heart. She heard how he talked against Israel, and mocked them. He would tell stories of how he had carried their maids captive to his city where he used them for a while, and then cast them off (Judges 5:30). And in her heart she despised him for it all. She easily perceived how filled with lust for women he was, and that he would have even seduced her, if he had the opportunity. Any wise woman can see the demon of lust in the eyes of a man who is driven by demonic desires. She had no respect for him. In fact, the more she listened to their conversation, the more she became sympathetic toward Israel. Many times she thought in her heart, "I wish I could do something to help Israel, but they know my husband is a friend of their enemy, and how could I ever expect them to trust me! Besides, what could I do; after all I am only a woman, and I am living in this tent day after day."

She was lonely for her family, from whom she was cut off, and because of their nomadic life she did not know when he would say, "Tomorrow we move to other pastures" and she would be the one to pack their things, fold their tents, and move on to the next green pasture.

As she watched Sisera nearing her tent, she knew her day had come to help Israel. She went out to meet him, and welcomed him, saying, "Come in, my Lord, come in to me; Don't be afraid."

Was she inviting him to more than a rest? Was she suggesting that she would yield to his previous sexual advances?

Some rabbinic scholars believe that Sisera took advantage of her invitation and abused her in a sexual way until he was exhausted, and because of his complete exhaustion, together with the milk she gave him to drink, he was caused to fall into a deep sleep, but not before he warned her that if anybody would come and ask if there was anybody in her tent she was to lie, and say, "No."

Something violent could have happened because, as soon as he was in a deep sleep, she hated him so much that only in a state of great anger and desire for retaliation could she have done what she did.

Covering him, so that he would not hear her movements, she fetched her hammer and one of the long, strong iron nails she had used to tie down the tent, and softly approached him. Her heart was beating wildly. What if he awakened? She knew he would kill her with one blow! He was a man of great anger and violence. A man who had respect for no one. But her contempt for him gave her courage.

Josephus says, "...when he was asleep, Jael took an iron nail, and with a hammer drove it through his temples into the floor."

The Bible says, *"Then Jael Heber's wife took a nail of the tent, and took an hammer in her hand, and went softly unto him, and smote the nail into his temples, and fastened it into the ground: for he was fast asleep and weary. So he died"* (Judges 4:21).

The sight of the smashed head and the blood spurting from it didn't appear to make her feel squeamish. She laid down her hammer and went to the door of the tent to wait for Barak. In her heart, she knew that he would soon appear. She could wait!

TRACING THE FOOTSTEPS OF BARAK

When Sisera fled for his life, Barak let him go; he went after the remnant of Sisera's army that was trying to escape, for he knew that God would use a woman to capture him.

We have to learn to let God use others. We do not need to do it all. Don't let Satan burden you down with responsibilities that belong to others. If you think you are the only one whom God can use, you will rob others of the opportunity of doing God's will and receiving eternal rewards. While it is true that often others cannot do as good a job as you can and their work may be far from perfect, you need to let them try, and if possible, lend a helping hand. There is a big difference between lending a helping hand, and taking the work away from them, and doing it yourself, because you feel it is inferior to your talents and capabilities. You are wronging yourself (by overburdening yourself with unnecessary responsibilities) and you are making others feel incapable, embarrassed and inferior to you. Sometimes the cruellest words you can say are, "Never mind, I'll do it myself!" Always allow others room to make mistakes.

This is what the clergy have done to women for the last two thousand years. The men have pushed the daughters of the Lord into the background, and made them feel inferior by rejecting them and the gifts and callings that lie dormant in their lives. As a result, the harvest has been dying unreaped in the fields of the world for generation after generation.

But, not only has the hierarchy of the Church perpetrated this against women, we women have often done it to each other, and so have the men. We have not encouraged one another to serve the Lord. There is too much jealousy and competition among God's children.

Barak pursued those who tried to escape the battle. He pursued them all the way to Harosheth of the Gentiles, and he didn't give up until *"all the host of Sisera fell upon the edge of the sword; and there was not a man left.*" Then he turned around and started looking for Sisera, himself.

When Barak and his men had slain the last of the "little guys," he turned and headed for Jael's tent. By now, he was so led and controlled by the Spirit of God, and so powerful in God, that he didn't need to have Deborah tell him what to do.

We may start out weak, but if we begin to do the will of God we will grow stronger in the battle because there is healing in the anointing. Many times I could have allowed myself to become an invalid, I felt so weak and weary and filled with pain, but I knew that if I could just get back in the pulpit, and let the anointing of God come upon me as I preached, that I would be strengthened physically through that anointing. Everything that touches the spirit touches the soul, and when the soul is inspired it breathes life into the flesh. We are a trinity, inseparably connected together. When our spirits are anointed, our souls are inspired, and they, in return, will give resurrection life to our bodies. Romans 8:11 says, "*But if the Spirit of him that raised up Jesus from the dead dwell in you, he that raised up Christ from the dead shall also quicken your mortal bodies by his Spirit that dwelleth in you"* (Romans 8:11).

Many servants of God have given up before their time, and ended their lives "on the shelf" of retired ministers of the Gospel. What a waste of talents, anointing, knowledge, and experience, which the Church urgently needed!

Burn, until you are totally burned out for God! Burn, until there is no flesh left! Burn, until the breath of God is reclaimed by God, Himself, and He takes you Home with the "kiss of death."

"BEHOLD, SISERA LAY DEAD!"

Barak seemed to be led by the Holy Spirit as he turned to run in the direction of Jael's tent. He ran like the wind; at times it seemed as though the wind was carrying him. He had never known such strength nor swiftness. He ran like the hind because, after all, a Naphtalite is a "hind let loose" and set free by the Holy Spirit. When a Naphtalite is anointed and endued with power from on high, he can run an obstacle race as though there were no obstacles nor hindrances in his path, he just glides over them. The mountains and hills are all joy to him. He views his enemies from the high places, and they suddenly become as small as ants.

The Wind of the Spirit takes Barak to the door of Jael's tent where he finds her waiting for him. Seeing him coming, she goes out to meet him, and says to him, "*Come, and I will shew thee the man whom thou seekest. And when he came into her tent, behold, Sisera lay dead, and the nail was in his temples*" (Judges 4:22).

Josephus says, "And when Barak came a little afterward, she shewed Sisera nailed to the ground: and thus was this victory gained by a woman, as Deborah had foretold."

Barak was not a hard-hearted man. He knew the enemy had to die, but the sight of how he had died shocked him. He looked at Sisera and then he looked at Jael. He knew that for this she could pay a great price. Her husband was sympathetic to the man she had slain. Everyone knew that. She had not been a good, obedient, submissive wife. She had been a wild woman, a wild goat from the mountains.

"How could you do it?" he asked. "Where did you get the strength?"

"Let me tell you," she answered. "Our people are nomads. We wander from place to place. Every time we arrive at a place where there is fresh pasture, it is my job, as a woman, to put up the tent before I start the evening meal. I am the one who has to do it. I unfold the tent, raise it, and tie its ropes to stakes that I have driven into the ground. It is hard work. Meanwhile, sometimes my husband does a little hunting, but mostly, he just sits there, waiting for me to get on with the job so I can make him and the household our evening meal. Many times, it has angered me to see him care so little that I was tired and worn-out from the journey, and I would swing that heavy hammer with the strength of anger. Through the years my muscles grew strong." She showed him the muscles of her right arm.

Barak looked at her with pity. This woman had suffered, but there was a greatness of God in her. She had used her difficulties and trials to make her strong. He couldn't help but admire her. He knew that she had no friends among his people, why then, did she do this for Israel? After all, she wasn't a "Jew."

"WHY DO YOU LOVE ISRAEL?"

That is the question the Jews ask us today. "Why do you come to Israel? Why aren't you afraid to come? Why do you want to live here among us? Why do you say you love us? Is it really true? Its hard to believe. You must have some other motive. Perhaps you want to proselytize us!"

They come to our conventions, and sit in amazement as they watch us sing the songs of Israel, and dance the Israeli dances, wave the Israeli flag and preach from their *Tenach*. Often we know their Bible better than the average Jew. We get up and say how much we love them. We raise money to bless and help them. Why?

Sometimes, we don't understand it ourselves. What is this strange love that we have in our hearts for "the Daughters of Jerusalem." Why do we identify ourselves with them? Why do we feel pain when they suffer? Why do we feel anger and grief when the world hates Israel and tries to destroy it?

We only know that God has put this special love in our hearts. Perhaps we are lost children of Jacob! Perhaps it is because God has touched our hearts with His love for His people. Or is it because we love a Certain Jew who gave His life for us long ago, and died that we might be "grafted into Israel" through faith in Him? If that is true, then, why do some who claim they too are His followers still hate His people? What is this thing, called Love for Israel?

And what about Jael? Was she, too, an Israelite woman who had married into the Kenite family of Heber? Moses had married a Kenite, why do we think it impossible that she might have done the same. What is the true secret of Jael? In the song of Deborah they applaud her, "*Blessed above women shall Jael the wife of Heber the Kenite be, blessed shall she be above women in the tent. He asked water, and she gave him milk; she brought forth butter in a lordly dish. She put her hand to the nail, and her right hand to the workmen's hammer; and with the hammer she smote Sisera, she smote off his head, when she had pierced and stricken through his temples. At her feet he bowed, he fell, he lay down: at her feet he bowed, he fell:*

where he bowed, there he fell down dead" (Judges 5:24-27).

Do not think of her as cruel, wondering why she could not have killed him in a more humane way! She used what she had. She used what she had been trained to use.

Perhaps, some day God will use your difficult hardships and the trials of your life to bring deliverance to Israel, and the nations of the world. God doesn't waste our sorrows. He doesn't waste our years of testings and pain and heartache. He doesn't waste anything! One day your tears will become your most beautiful rainbows!

GO AFTER THE RULING SPIRITS

Barak walked out of the tent. He knew his work was not over. The victory was not final, Jael had rid Israel of their great enemy, Sisera; but there was one more deadly and dangerous enemy, King Jabin, who was still living in the stronghold of Hazor, the city whose name means "secure, fully protected, stronghold."

Barak determined he would not leave this task to a woman! Nor to anyone else! He moved like lightning, because, after all, that is what the name "Barak" means, and he had come into his destiny.

Josephus tells the rest of the story, "Barak also fought with Jabin at Hazor; and when he met with him, he slew him."

It is not enough to cast out all the small demons, one must go after the ruling spirit that has control over all the others. As long as he remains in control he will soon call back other spirits to return to the person whom they are tormenting and destroying.

The war isn't won until you get your "Hitler," himself. And even then, it is not completely over until you destroy the spirit of Naziism, because it will rise again later. That is what is happening in Germany and some of the nations of the world today. Often it resurrected by another name, but it is the same spirit of Fascism, and it will destroy others with its cruel totalitarian control of others.

There are territorial ruling spirits over lands which we have never dealt with, and so, even though we may set a generation free during a great revival, still, when that generation passes on, the next one will have to contend with the ruling spirits. That is why revivals pass into history, and great moves of God die out, like they did in Wales, and many other places. That is also the reason why some moves of God that were pure to begin with, turn into error and become cults.

Don't stop fighting until the battle is over. Never compromise with evil. If you do, you or your children will have to face your enemy, or his son, ten years later when he is stronger. These are the days in which many false peace treaties are being negotiated. None of them will last, because we have not gotten to the root cause of the trouble. We are only wrestling with flesh and blood when there are *"principalities, powers, the rulers of the darkness of this world and spiritual wickedness in high places"* (Ephesians 6:12).

Only prayer and fasting and spiritual warfare through holy lives will solve the problems of the Middle East. There are no answers at any "round tables" of discussion by unregenerate and prejudiced people who themselves are under the influence of these evil powers that rule over nations.

That is why we have founded houses of prayer in Jerusalem and Galilee. We know that we must be watchmen on the wall for Israel through the power of the Holy Spirit. We believe that God will hear our prayers and the devil will hear our praises, and we will dislodge him from his stronghold and bring victory and peace to Israel.

The story of Deborah closes with the words of Josephus, "Barak overthrew the city Hazor to its foundation, and was the commander of the Israelites for forty years."

The stronghold of the enemy had been destroyed under Joshua over a hundred years earlier. Just because we got rid of the enemy in the past, does not mean that he will not try again to take over if we give him any leeway through sin, like Israel did when she forsook the Lord and turned to other gods. Sin opens the door to Satan. He is a legalist. He is always watching us, and has his demons spying for him, and advising him. If we allow sin to have dominion over us, we open the gate for Satan to come immediately with sickness, depression, poverty, disunity, separation, divorce, and many other destructive evils. Only by crawling back to Jesus on our hands and knees, and flinging ourselves at the foot of the cross, and confessing our sins with a broken and contrite heart, can we break the power of sin's retribution off our lives, for it is true that *"The wages of sin is death; but the gift of God is eternal life through Jesus Christ our Lord"* (Romans 6:23).

When Israel repented of her sin and cried to God, He raised up Deborah, who called out Barak to lead the nation to liberation.

In these days, when iniquity is ever increasing, both in the world and in the Church, God will raise up many prophets and prophetesses, many warriors, and housewives, like Jael, who will be used of God to warn the people, save souls, restore the Church, and prepare the Bride of Christ for the coming of the Lord.

You may not feel that you can ever be a prophetess like Deborah, or the commander of an army, like Barak; but if you are a "housewife," or a "carpenter" who knows how to "swing a hammer" God has a place for you in His plan; and He will use you now.

Barak became Commander over Israel for the next forty years, and God's people lived in peace and safety.

DEBORAH AND BARAK'S SONG OF THANKSGIVING

This story would not be complete if we did not read again the Song of Deborah from Judges chapter five, and take time to meditate on it:

1 Then sang Deborah and Barak the son of Abinoam on that day, saying,

2 Praise ye the LORD for the avenging of Israel, when the people willingly offered themselves.

3 Hear, O ye kings; give ear, O ye princes; I, even I, will sing unto the LORD; I will sing praise to the LORD God of Israel.

4 LORD, when thou wentest out of Seir, when thou marchedst out of the field of Edom, the earth trembled, and the heavens dropped, the clouds also dropped water.

5 The mountains melted from before the LORD, even that Sinai from before the LORD God of Israel.

6 In the days of Shamgar the son of Anath, in the days of Jael, the highways were unoccupied, and the travellers walked through byways.

7 The inhabitants of the villages ceased, they ceased in Israel, until that I Deborah arose, that I arose a mother in Israel.

8 They chose new gods; then was war in the gates: was there a shield or spear seen among forty thousand in Israel?

9 My heart is toward the governors of Israel, that offered themselves willingly among the people. Bless ye the LORD.

10 Speak, ye that ride on white asses, ye that sit in judgment, and walk by the way.

11 They that are delivered from the noise of archers in the places of drawing water, there shall they rehearse the righteous acts of the LORD, even the righteous acts toward the inhabitants of his villages in Israel: then shall the people of the LORD go down to the gates.

12 Awake, awake, Deborah: awake, awake, utter a song: arise, Barak, and lead thy captivity captive, thou son of Abinoam.

13 Then he made him that remaineth have dominion over the nobles among the people: the LORD made me have dominion over the mighty.

14 Out of EPHRAIM was there a root of them against Amalek; after thee, BENJAMIN, among thy people; out of MACHIR [MANASSEH] *came down governors, and out of ZEBULUN they that handle the pen of the writer.*

15 And the princes of ISSACHAR were with Deborah; even Issachar, and also Barak: he was sent on foot into the valley. For the divisions of REUBEN there were great thoughts of heart.

16 Why abodest thou among the sheepfolds, to hear the bleatings of the flocks? For the divisions of REUBEN there were great searchings of heart.

17 GILEAD [GAD] *abode beyond Jordan: and why did DAN remain in ships? ASHER continued on the sea shore, and abode in his breaches.*

18 ZEBULUN and NAPHTALI were a people that jeoparded their lives unto the death in the high places of the field.

19 The kings came and fought, then fought the kings of Canaan in Taanach by the waters of Megiddo; they took no gain of money.

20 They fought from heaven; the stars in their courses fought against Sisera.

21 The river of Kishon swept them away, that ancient river, the river Kishon. O my soul, thou hast trodden down strength.

22 Then were the horsehoofs broken by the means of the pransings, the pransings of their mighty ones.

23 Curse ye Meroz, said the angel of the LORD, curse ye bitterly the inhabitants thereof; because they came not to the help of the LORD, to the help of the LORD against the mighty.

24 Blessed above women shall Jael the wife of Heber the Kenite be, blessed shall she be above women in the tent.

25 He asked water, and she gave him milk; she brought forth butter in a lordly dish.

26 She put her hand to the nail, and her right hand to the workmen's hammer; and with the hammer she smote Sisera, she smote off his head, when she had pierced and stricken through his temples.

27 At her feet he bowed, he fell, he lay down: at her feet he bowed, he fell: where he bowed, there he fell down dead.

28 The mother of Sisera looked out at a window, and cried through the lattice, Why is his chariot so long in coming? why tarry the wheels of his chariots?

29 Her wise ladies answered her, yea, she returned answer to herself,

30 Have they not sped? have they not divided the prey; to every man a damsel or two; to Sisera a prey of divers colours, a prey of divers colours of needlework, of divers colours of needlework on both sides, meet for the necks of them that take the spoil?

31 So let all thine enemies perish, O LORD: but let them that love him be as the sun when he goeth forth in his might. And the land had rest forty years.

The End

THE MEANING OF NAMES OF PEOPLE AND PLACES IN THE STORY

BARAK: lightening

DEBORAH: bee

HAROSHETH: mechanical works, carving, cutting, smithy

HAZOR: secure, fully protected

HEBER: charmer

JABIN: that wise one

JAEL: wild goat

KEDESH: sanctuary

LAPIDOTH: to shine, lamp, flame, burning lamp, torch

SISERA: militant, warlord.

More Life-Changing Books

Gwen Shaw's Autobiography

UNCONDITIONAL SURRENDER. The life story of Gwen R. Shaw, lovingly known as "Sister Gwen" to thousands of people in over one hundred nations. You will laugh and cry with her as you feel the heartbeat of a great woman of God who has given all to Him, asking only for souls in return. Your life will be challenged as you walk with her through mission field after mission field. You will never be the same when you read how God pours out His Spirit and confirms His Word.

Paperback .... #000102 $14.00
Video NTSC (North American format) .... #GSL-99 $20.00
Video PAL (European format) .... #GSLP-99 $20.00

Daily Devotionals by Gwen Shaw

DAILY PREPARATIONS FOR PERFECTION — This daily devotional comes to you exactly as the Holy Spirit spoke to the author's heart in her own private devotions. You will feel that Jesus is speaking to you every time you open it. It is loved by all. You'll read it and re-read it.
.... Paperback #000202 $12.50

DAY BY DAY— This daily devotional book based on the Psalms will give you an inspiring word directly from the Throne Room each day to fill your heart with praise to God. Starting each day with praise is the secret of a joy-filled life .... Softcover #000204 $9.95
.... Hardcover #000203 $18.50
Also available in French .... Hardcover #000203FR $18.50

FROM THE HEART OF JESUS — This devotional book will take you back to Bible days and you will walk and talk with Jesus and His disciples as he ministered to the people, as He suffered and died and as He rose again from the dead. These words from the heart of Jesus will go straight to your heart, bringing comfort, peace, encouragement and hope! 923 pages .... Hardcover #000207 $29.95

IT'S TIME FOR REVIVAL. A Bible study on revival that not only gives scriptural promises of the end-time revival, but also presents the stories of revivals in the past and the revivalists whom God used. It will stir your heart and encourage you to believe for great revival! ....#000311 $7.75

OUR MINISTERING ANGELS. A scriptural Bible study on the topic of angels. Angels will be playing a more and more prominent part in these last days. We need to understand about them and their ministry. Read exciting accounts of angelic help ....#000308 $8.00

POUR OUT YOUR HEART. A wonderful Bible study on travailing prayer. The hour has come to intercede before the throne of God. The call to intercession is for everyone, and we must carry the Lord's burden and weep for the lost so that the harvest can be brought in quickly. ....#000301 $5.00

REDEEMING THE LAND. A Bible study on spiritual warfare. This important teaching will help you know your authority through the Blood of Jesus to dislodge evil spirits, break the curse, and restore God's blessing upon the land. ....#000309 $9.50

THE FINE LINE. This Bible study clearly magnifies the "fine line" of difference between the soul realm and the spirit realm. Both are intangible and therefore cannot be discerned with the five senses, but must be discerned by the Holy Spirit and the Word of God. A must for the deeper Christian ....#000307 $6.00

THE POWER OF THE PRECIOUS BLOOD. A Bible study on the Blood of Jesus. The author shares how it was revealed to her how much Satan fears Jesus' Blood. This Bible study will help you overcome and destroy the works of Satan in your life and the lives of loved ones! ....#000303 $5.00

THE POWER OF PRAISE. When God created the heavens and the earth, He was surrounded by praise. Miracles happen when holy people praise a Holy God! Praise is the language of creation. If prayer can move the hand of God, how much more praise can move Him! ....#000312 $5.00

YE SHALL RECEIVE POWER FROM ON HIGH. This is a much needed foundational teaching on the Baptism of the Holy Spirit. It will enable you to teach this subject, as well as to understand these truths more fully yourself..#000310 $5.00

YOUR APPOINTMENT WITH GOD. A Bible study on fasting. Fasting is one of the most neglected sources of power over bondages of Satan that God has given the Church. The author's experiences shared in this Bible study will change your life..............................#000302 $5.00

IN-DEPTH STUDIES FOR THE SERIOUS BIBLE STUDENT

FORGIVE AND RECEIVE. This Bible Study is a lesson to the church on the much-needed truths of forgiveness and restoration. The epistle to Philemon came from the heart of Paul who had experienced great forgiveness...#000406 $7.00

GRACE ALONE. This study teaches the reader to gain freedom in the finished work of the Cross by forsaking works (which cannot add to salvation) and live by ***Grace Alone***............................#000402 $13.00

MYSTERY REVEALED. Search the depths of God's riches in one of Paul's most profound epistles, "to the praise of His glory!" Learn the "mystery" of the united Body of Christ..#000403 $15.00

OUR GLORIOUS HEAD. This book teaches vital truths for today, assisting the reader in discerning false teachings, when the philosophies of men are being promoted as being the truths of God. Jesus Christ is the Head of His Body!............................#000404 $9.00

THE CATCHING AWAY! This is a very timely Bible study because Jesus is coming soon! The book of 1 Thessalonians explains God's revelation to Paul on the rapture of the saints. 2 Thessalonians reveals what will happen after the rapture when the antichrist takes over. ....#000407 $13.00

THE LOVE LETTER. This expository study of the letter to the first church of Europe will give the reader an understanding of Paul's great love for the church that was born out of his suffering. ....#000405 $9.00

POPULAR BIBLE COURSE

THE TRIBES OF ISRAEL. This popular and well-loved study on the thirteen tribes of Israel will show you your place in the spiritual tribes in these last days. Understand yourself and others better through the study of this Bible Course! ....#000501 $45.00
....Set of 13 tapes #TGS1 $42.00

THE WOMEN OF THE BIBLE SERIES BY GWEN SHAW, opens a window into the lives of the women of the Bible in the style of historical novels. Their joys and heartaches were the same as ours today.

EVE—MOTHER OF US ALL. Read the life story of the first woman. Discover the secrets of one of the most neglected and misunderstood stories in history ....#000801 $4.50

SARAH—PRINCESS OF ALL MANKIND. She was beautiful — and barren. Feel the heartbeat and struggles of this woman who left so great an impact on us all ....#000802 $4.50

REBEKAH—THE BRIDE. The destiny of the world was determined when she said three simple words, "I will go!" Enjoy this touching story. ....#000803 $4.50

LEAH AND RACHEL—THE TWIN WIVES OF JACOB. You will feel their dreams, their pains, their jealousies and their love for one man. ....#000804 $4.50

MIRIAM—THE PROPHETESS. Miriam was the first female to lead worship, the first woman to whom the Lord gave the title "Leader of God's people." ....#000805 $7.50

Other Books by Gwen Shaw

GOING HOME. This book is a treasure which answers so many questions and comforts so many hearts. It gives strength and faith, and helps one to cope with the pain of the loss of a loved one. This book is not really a book about dying, but about Going Home to our Eternal Abode with our loving Heavenly Father ....#000607 $8.00

KEEPING GOD'S SECRETS *"The secret of the Lord is with them that fear Him; and He will shew them His covenant"* Psalm 25:14. When the Lord knows that He can trust us with His secrets, He will reveal things to us which He cannot reveal to others...............#000608 $7.00

LOVE, THE LAW OF THE ANGELS. This is undoubtedly the greatest of Gwen Shaw's writings. It carries a message of healing and life in a sad and fallen civilization. Love heals the broken-hearted and sets disarray in order. You will never be the same after reading this beautiful book about love. ....#000601 $10.00

SONG OF LOVE. She was a heart-broken missionary, far from home. She cried out to God for help. He spoke, "Turn to the Song of Solomon and read!" As she turned in obedience, the Lord took her into the "Throne Room" of Heaven and taught her about the love of Christ for His Bride, the church. She fell in love with Jesus afresh, and you will too ....#000401 $7.50

THE FALSE FAST. Now, from the pen of Gwen Shaw, author of Your Appointment With God (a Bible Study on fasting), comes an exposé on the False Fast. It will help you to examine your motives for fasting, and make your foundations sure, so that your fast will be a potent tool in the hands of God .... #000602 $2.50

THE LIGHT WILL COME FROM RUSSIA. The thrilling testimony of Mother Barbara, Abbess of the Mount of Olives in Jerusalem. She shares prophecies which were given to her concerning the nations of the world in our time by a holy bishop of the Kremlin, just prior to the Russian Revolution .... #000606 $5.50

THE PARABLE OF THE GOLDEN RAIN. This is the story of how revivals come and go, and a true picture, in parable language, of how the Church tries to replace the genuine move of the Spirit with man-made programs and tactics. It's amusing and convicting at the same time .... #000603 $4.00

THEY SHALL MOUNT UP WITH WINGS AS EAGLES. Though you may feel old or tired, if you wait on the Lord, you shall mount up on wings as eagles! Let this book encourage you to stretch your wings and fulfill your destiny — no matter what your age! .... #000604 $6.95

TO BE LIKE JESUS. Based on her Throne Room experience in 1971, the author shares the Father's heart about our place as sons in His Family. Nothing is more important than To Be Like Jesus! .... #000605 $6.95

Pocket Sermon Books by Gwen Shaw

BEHOLD, THIS DREAMER COMETH. Dreams and dreamers are God's gift to humanity to bring His purposes into the hearts of mankind. The life of Joseph, the dreamer, will encourage you to believe God to fulfill the dream He has put into your heart .... #000707 $2.00

BREAKTHROUGH. Just like when Peter was in prison, sometimes you need a "breakthrough" in your life! This book reveals the truth in a fresh and living way! .... #000708 $2.00

DON'T STRIKE THE ROCK! When Moses became angry with the people's rebellion and disobeyed God's order to speak to the Rock, it cost him his entrance into the Promised Land. Don't allow anything to keep you from fulfilling God's perfect will for your life!...#000704 $2.00

GOD WILL DESTROY THE VEIL OF BLINDNESS. "...as the veil of the Temple was rent...I shall again rend the veil in two....for...the Arab, so they shall know that I am God...." This was the word of the Lord concerning God's plan for the nations in the days to come. Join in with Abraham's prayer "Let Ishmael live before Thee!" ....#000712 $2.00

HASTENING OUR REDEMPTION. All of Heaven and Earth are waiting for the Body of Christ to rise up in maturity and reclaim what we lost in the Fall of Man. Applying the Blood of Jesus is the key to *Hastening Our Redemption* ....#000705 $2.00

IT CAN BE AVERTED. Many people today are burdened and fearful over prophecies of doom and destruction. However, the Bible is clear that God prefers mercy over judgment when His people humble themselves and pray ....#000706 $2.00

IT'S TIME FOR CHANGE. After Sept. 11, '01, everyone has agreed that "Things will never be the same!" And they aren't! But the evil that was released on that day is not the only change. There also are positive changes taking place. Thank God! The Almighty is still on the throne, and nothing can happen which He does not permit!
....#000713 $2.00

KAIROS TIME. That once in a lifetime opportunity—that second, or minute, or hour, or year, or even longer, when a golden opportunity is sovereignly given to us by the Almighty. What we do with it can change our lives and possibly even change the world...............#000709 $2.00

KNOWING ONE ANOTHER IN THE SPIRIT. Experience great peace as you learn to understand the difficulties your friends, enemies and loved ones face that help to form their character. "Wherefore henceforth know we no man after the flesh..." (II Cor. 5:16a) ....#000703 $2.00

THE ANOINTING BREAKS THE YOKE. Learn how the anointing of God can set you free from your bondage: free to fulfill your destiny in the call of God on your life! ....#000710 $2.00

THE CHURCH OF THE OPEN ARMS. It is time to ask God for the nations. But how can we when we have so little love for others? We need to ask God to enlarge our hearts to make us a blessing. Open your heart and open your arms! ....#000714 $2.00

THE CRUCIFIED LIFE. When you suffer, knowing the cause is not your own sin, for you have searched your heart before God, then you must accept that it is God doing a new thing in your life. Let joy rise up within you because you are a partaker of Christ's suffering....#000701 $2.00

THE MASTER IS COME AND CALLETH FOR THEE. Read about how the Lord called Gwen Shaw to begin the ministry of the End-Time Handmaidens and Servants. Perhaps the Master is also calling you into His service. Bring Him the fragments of your life — He will put them together again. An anointed message booklet ....#000702 $2.00

THE MERCY SEAT. The Days of Grace are coming to a close, and the Days of Mercy are now here. And oh, how we need mercy! There never has been a time when we needed it more!...........#000711 $2.00

CHILDREN'S BOOKS BY GWEN SHAW

LITTLE ONES TO HIM BELONG. Based on the testimonies of children's visions of Heaven and the death of a small Chinese boy, Sister Gwen weaves a delightful story of the precious joys of Heaven for children of all ages ....#000901 $9.00

TELL ME THE STORIES OF JESUS. Some of the greatest New Testament stories of the Life of Jesus and written in a way that will interest children and help them to love Jesus ....#000902 $9.00